# MAMA'S BABY JOURNAL

*A Keepsake for*
## PRECIOUS MEMORIES, MOMENTS, MILESTONES, AND MIRACLES

JENNIFER BASYE SANDER

Skyhorse Publis

T0306576

*Dedicated to:*

_____

Your favorite photo of Mama and baby

# Contents

# *Introduction*

s there a baby in your future? Congratulations! These next few days, weeks, months, and all the years to come will be the adventure of a lifetime, filled with love, wonder, and . . . maybe a bump or two.

When I began creating this memory journal, my first worry was that my two boys are no longer babies; I'm pretty far down the path of motherhood. Maybe it should be written by a mom with a more recent experience. . . .

But then I thought, *Well, who better to compile a book than a parent who misses those sweet little moments of joy?* My sons Julian and Pips are off doing their own young-man thing these days, mostly turning up when they are hungry. How I would love for just a few more of those cuddly afternoons on a couch with a toddler, or the soft murmur of a baby's voice in the morning.

I also reached out to other moms whose children are long past the young years to ask, "What do you most regret not writing down? What moments do you wish you could relive? What would you tell a new parent about preserving those moments?"

Here is the one thing I do know as an experienced mom: Whatever your journaling goals are, you should cut yourself some slack. There is no perfect way to do any of this, just as there is no perfect way to make a family. Families are created through pregnancy, adoption, surrogacy, step-parenthood—there is not one set way to hang on to the memories. Sometimes you may write every day, other times you may set this journal aside for weeks, months, maybe even years. And that is fine. Think of this journal as an old friend encouraging you to capture what you can when you can. Savor the time that you can sit down and fill these pages, but skip the guilt if it has been awhile since your last entry. Because hey, you're busy, right? You're a mom. Welcome to the journey!

# How to Use This Journal

**T**his might well be the first time that you have tried to journal. If so, relax. No one is looking over your shoulder here, no one will be grading your grammar, spelling, or sentence structure. Let's think about a few things first, though.

Some of these pages are places to list factual information and data, such as a record of your doctor appointments or who gave you the hand-knitted booties at a baby shower. On other pages though, you will find space to reflect more deeply on your motherhood journey. No matter how much you vow to write regularly, you will not always have the time to write much, particularly with a newborn baby. So when that happens just jot a note or two to yourself on the page and come back to fill in more whenever you can. There are no deadlines here.

But who, exactly, is your audience? Sometimes you will be writing to yourself, sometimes to your child. Or you might be addressing some future descendant. Don't worry about consistency; just go ahead and put your thoughts and observations and feelings down on the page without feeling the weight of perfection. In fact, don't worry about who the audience is. Right this minute it is an audience of one—you. So make sure that you are there on the page along with your baby.

And how boldly honest do you want to be about what your life and emotions are like right now? It is entirely up to you. There might be times when instead of writing in the book you write on a blank sheet of paper and tuck it inside the journal to be reviewed again at a later date. Upon further reflection, you can write it into the journal or wad up the paper and toss it if you no longer want those exact thoughts to be recorded.

Other than events in your own daily life, is this a place to record a glimpse of what is happening in the world around you? You can, if you wish, use this journal to leave an historical record for your future descendants. Just as our generation enjoys looking at old photos from the twentieth century or goofy sixties and seventies Polaroids (did they really wear those pants?!), your child might someday have a child who will read with great interest about what was swirling around you in the first quarter of the twenty-first century.

# Anticipation

A baby is on the way!
These next nine months will be filled with anticipation.

# Becoming a Mother

When I thought about having children, I imagined that:

...........................................................................................

...........................................................................................

...........................................................................................

...........................................................................................

...........................................................................................

...........................................................................................

And I'd name you . . .

...........................................................................................

...........................................................................................

...........................................................................................

...........................................................................................

...........................................................................................

...........................................................................................

# The Moment I Found Out about You

The first person I told was:

........................................................................................................................

........................................................................................................................

........................................................................................................................

........................................................................................................................

........................................................................................................................

........................................................................................................................

And then I told:

........................................................................................................................

........................................................................................................................

........................................................................................................................

........................................................................................................................

........................................................................................................................

# My First Few Months

The biggest challenge was:

........................................................................................................................................

........................................................................................................................................

........................................................................................................................................

........................................................................................................................................

........................................................................................................................................

........................................................................................................................................

........................................................................................................................................

........................................................................................................................................

........................................................................................................................................

........................................................................................................................................

........................................................................................................................................

........................................................................................................................................

# I Saw You for the First Time

An ultrasound, and there you were!

..................................................................................................
..................................................................................................
..................................................................................................
..................................................................................................
..................................................................................................
..................................................................................................

Who else was there?

..................................................................................................
..................................................................................................
..................................................................................................
..................................................................................................
..................................................................................................
..................................................................................................

*Glue or tape in a copy of your ultrasound picture*

"The first time I was pregnant, pie was all I could think about. Seriously. Even on hot summer days I wanted a warm slice of pie." —Beanie, mother of two

There might be mixed emotions around sharing about a pregnancy. "I knew I should have felt joy," said Jenna Bush Hager on discovering she was going to have a third baby. "But my first feeling was a surge of survivor's guilt. Many of my friends were struggling with infertility. How would they take the news that I was going to have a surprise baby?"

"I mean, wouldn't you rather laugh than cry? When you're pregnant, you often want to cry, you often want to yell . . . your emotions are going crazy because of all the hormonal changes." —Jenny McCarthy

# I Got Advice from Friends and Relatives

Some of it was practical:

......................................................................................................................

......................................................................................................................

......................................................................................................................

......................................................................................................................

......................................................................................................................

......................................................................................................................

Some of it was kind of kooky:

......................................................................................................................

......................................................................................................................

......................................................................................................................

......................................................................................................................

......................................................................................................................

......................................................................................................................

# My Doctor's Appointments

My OB/GYN doctor was:

...................................................................................................

...................................................................................................

...................................................................................................

My appointments:

...................................................................................................

...................................................................................................

...................................................................................................

...................................................................................................

...................................................................................................

...................................................................................................

...................................................................................................

...................................................................................................

...................................................................................................

# Pregnancy Cravings

What I most wanted was:

.................................................................................................................

.................................................................................................................

.................................................................................................................

.................................................................................................................

But all of a sudden I didn't like:

.................................................................................................................

.................................................................................................................

.................................................................................................................

.................................................................................................................

And I *really* couldn't stand:

.................................................................................................................

.................................................................................................................

.................................................................................................................

.................................................................................................................

# There Was a Baby Shower

Guests:

..............................................    ..............................................    ..............................................

..............................................    ..............................................    ..............................................

..............................................    ..............................................    ..............................................

..............................................    ..............................................    ..............................................

..............................................    ..............................................    ..............................................

Games:

..............................................    ..............................................

..............................................    ..............................................

..............................................    ..............................................

..............................................    ..............................................

..............................................    ..............................................

*Be sure to include your
favorite pictures from
your baby shower*

Gifts:

........................................  ........................................  ........................................

........................................  ........................................  ........................................

........................................  ........................................  ........................................

........................................  ........................................  ........................................

........................................  ........................................  ........................................

........................................  ........................................  ........................................

........................................  ........................................  ........................................

........................................  ........................................

........................................  ........................................

........................................  ........................................

# What I Wore

My clothes stopped fitting eventually . . .

........................................................................................................................................

........................................................................................................................................

........................................................................................................................................

........................................................................................................................................

Maternity clothes, bought or borrowed?

........................................................................................................................................

........................................................................................................................................

........................................................................................................................................

........................................................................................................................................

My favorite thing to wear was:

........................................................................................................................................

........................................................................................................................................

........................................................................................................................................

........................................................................................................................................

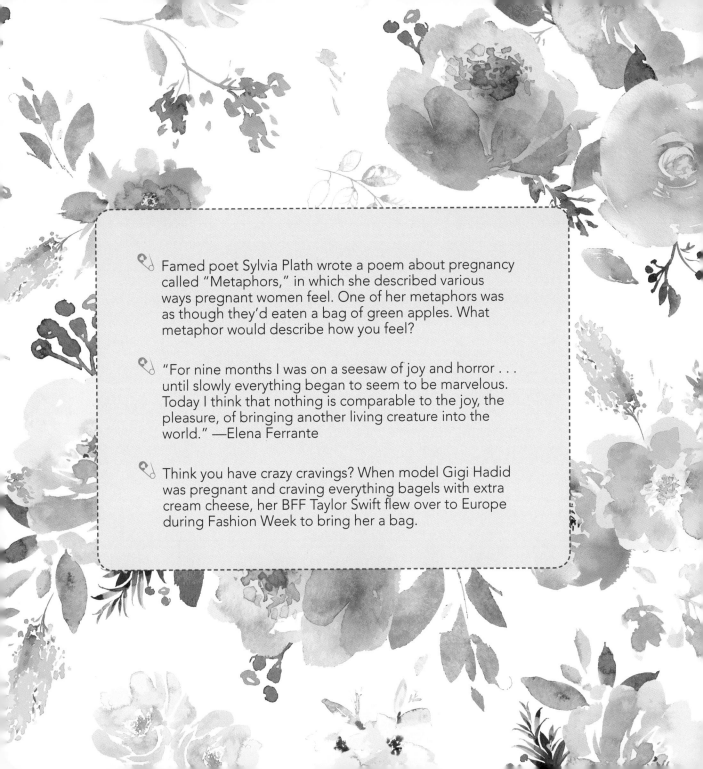

Famed poet Sylvia Plath wrote a poem about pregnancy called "Metaphors," in which she described various ways pregnant women feel. One of her metaphors was as though they'd eaten a bag of green apples. What metaphor would describe how you feel?

"For nine months I was on a seesaw of joy and horror . . . until slowly everything began to seem to be marvelous. Today I think that nothing is comparable to the joy, the pleasure, of bringing another living creature into the world." —Elena Ferrante

Think you have crazy cravings? When model Gigi Hadid was pregnant and craving everything bagels with extra cream cheese, her BFF Taylor Swift flew over to Europe during Fashion Week to bring her a bag.

# You Began to Move Inside of Me!

Where I first felt you move:

.................................................................................................................................

.................................................................................................................................

.................................................................................................................................

.................................................................................................................................

.................................................................................................................................

Who else felt you moving:

.................................................................................................................................

.................................................................................................................................

.................................................................................................................................

.................................................................................................................................

.................................................................................................................................

.................................................................................................................................

# Birth Classes

My birthing class partner was:

........................................................................................

........................................................................................

........................................................................................

........................................................................................

The instructor was:

........................................................................................

........................................................................................

........................................................................................

........................................................................................

What I remember most from what I learned:

........................................................................................

........................................................................................

........................................................................................

........................................................................................

# Outfitting Your Nursery

Borrowed or loaned baby items:

.................................................................................................................

.................................................................................................................

.................................................................................................................

.................................................................................................................

Here are a few things I bought just for you:

.................................................................................................................

.................................................................................................................

.................................................................................................................

.................................................................................................................

Paint, wallpaper, and fabrics:

.........................................................................................

.........................................................................................

.........................................................................................

.........................................................................................

*Add photos of your nursery, or fabric samples, paint strips, etc.!*

# I'm Getting Closer . . .

Lately I've been feeling:

.................................................................................................

.................................................................................................

.................................................................................................

Early plans that have already changed:

.................................................................................................

.................................................................................................

.................................................................................................

What I've been most surprised by is:

.................................................................................................

.................................................................................................

.................................................................................................

What I've been most delighted by is:

.................................................................................................

.................................................................................................

.................................................................................................

# Spring, Summer, Autumn, Winter . . .

While I was pregnant, the weather was:

....................................................................................................

....................................................................................................

....................................................................................................

....................................................................................................

....................................................................................................

....................................................................................................

....................................................................................................

I most enjoyed the days when:

....................................................................................................

....................................................................................................

....................................................................................................

....................................................................................................

....................................................................................................

....................................................................................................

....................................................................................................

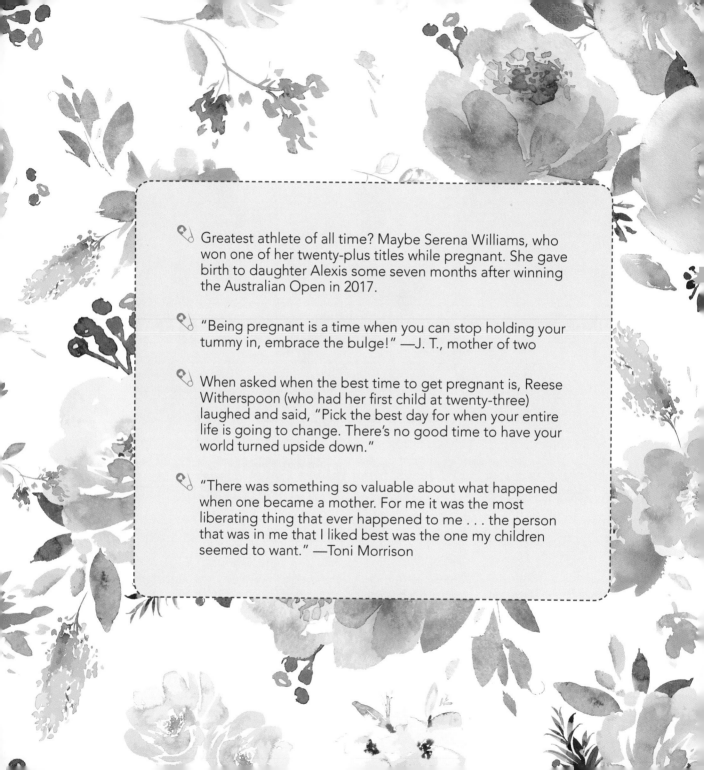

Greatest athlete of all time? Maybe Serena Williams, who won one of her twenty-plus titles while pregnant. She gave birth to daughter Alexis some seven months after winning the Australian Open in 2017.

"Being pregnant is a time when you can stop holding your tummy in, embrace the bulge!" —J. T., mother of two

When asked when the best time to get pregnant is, Reese Witherspoon (who had her first child at twenty-three) laughed and said, "Pick the best day for when your entire life is going to change. There's no good time to have your world turned upside down."

"There was something so valuable about what happened when one became a mother. For me it was the most liberating thing that ever happened to me . . . the person that was in me that I liked best was the one my children seemed to want." —Toni Morrison

# My Birth Plans

Using a coach, midwife, or doula?

............................................................................................................................

............................................................................................................................

Which hospital I will head to:

............................................................................................................................

............................................................................................................................

Planning a homebirth?

............................................................................................................................

............................................................................................................................

Any special arrangements?

............................................................................................................................

............................................................................................................................

Anyone else invited to the birth?

............................................................................................................................

............................................................................................................................

# It's Dream Time . . .

How pregnancy affected my sleep:

......................................................................................................................................

......................................................................................................................................

......................................................................................................................................

Dreams while pregnant:

......................................................................................................................................

......................................................................................................................................

......................................................................................................................................

*Picture of you while pregnant*

# The Naming Game

Names we considered:

..................................................................................................................

..................................................................................................................

Names we rejected:

..................................................................................................................

..................................................................................................................

We finally chose:

..................................................................................................................

..................................................................................................................

And you got your name because:

..................................................................................................................

..................................................................................................................

..................................................................................................................

# Babymoons

A lot of couples like to take their last chance to travel as just the two of them before the baby comes. Did you travel or take any trips while pregnant?

..................................................................................................................................

..................................................................................................................................

..................................................................................................................................

..................................................................................................................................

..................................................................................................................................

..................................................................................................................................

..................................................................................................................................

..................................................................................................................................

..................................................................................................................................

..................................................................................................................................

..................................................................................................................................

..................................................................................................................................

..................................................................................................................................

..................................................................................................................................

# Packing the Hospital Bag

Here is what I thought I'd need:

........................................................................................................

........................................................................................................

........................................................................................................

........................................................................................................

........................................................................................................

........................................................................................................

........................................................................................................

Here is what I actually used!

........................................................................................................

........................................................................................................

........................................................................................................

........................................................................................................

........................................................................................................

........................................................................................................

........................................................................................................

# Reflections: Family Origins

Do you know how your family came to be here? How much of your family story has been passed down? Are there old country traditions that are still evident in your family?

..........................................................................................................................

..........................................................................................................................

..........................................................................................................................

..........................................................................................................................

..........................................................................................................................

..........................................................................................................................

..........................................................................................................................

..........................................................................................................................

..........................................................................................................................

..........................................................................................................................

..........................................................................................................................

..........................................................................................................................

..........................................................................................................................

# Reflections: Family Traditions

Are there holiday or other traditions you would like to preserve? And are there any you'd like to see disappear?

........................................................................................................

........................................................................................................

........................................................................................................

........................................................................................................

........................................................................................................

........................................................................................................

Birthday traditions:

........................................................................................................

........................................................................................................

........................................................................................................

........................................................................................................

........................................................................................................

What is your favorite holiday meal? Do you know how to make it? Write the recipe here:

...........................................................................................................................

...........................................................................................................................

...........................................................................................................................

...........................................................................................................................

...........................................................................................................................

...........................................................................................................................

...........................................................................................................................

...........................................................................................................................

Singing is an ancient ritual. Do you have a favorite holiday song? Do you know all of the words? Will you be able to teach it to your child? And who taught you? Write the words down here:

...........................................................................................................................

...........................................................................................................................

...........................................................................................................................

...........................................................................................................................

...........................................................................................................................

...........................................................................................................................

...........................................................................................................................

...........................................................................................................................

# Reflections: Holiday Time

Mom-to-be, are you expecting at the same time you are getting ready for a big annual holiday? Easter, Christmas, Kwanza, Hanukkah, Ramadan? All year-round there are big dates that might make you feel extra emotional as childhood holiday memories come flooding back. So why not write down a few here, along with how you anticipate sharing the holiday with your child next year . . .

What is your favorite yearly holiday?

.......................................................................................................................

.......................................................................................................................

.......................................................................................................................

.......................................................................................................................

.......................................................................................................................

Describe your most treasured holiday memory:

.......................................................................................................................

.......................................................................................................................

.......................................................................................................................

.......................................................................................................................

What do you most look forward to doing with your child next year when your favorite holiday rolls around?

..........................................................................................................

..........................................................................................................

..........................................................................................................

..........................................................................................................

..........................................................................................................

..........................................................................................................

..........................................................................................................

..........................................................................................................

..........................................................................................................

..........................................................................................................

..........................................................................................................

..........................................................................................................

..........................................................................................................

..........................................................................................................

..........................................................................................................

# Reflections: My Pregnancy Experience

How would you sum up these past nine months? What are some moments of delight? Have there been unexpected challenges?

.......................................................................................................................................

.......................................................................................................................................

.......................................................................................................................................

.......................................................................................................................................

.......................................................................................................................................

.......................................................................................................................................

.......................................................................................................................................

.......................................................................................................................................

.......................................................................................................................................

.......................................................................................................................................

.......................................................................................................................................

.......................................................................................................................................

# Arrival

The baby is coming!

# Due Dates vs. Reality

Your due date was meant to be:

........................................................................................

........................................................................................

........................................................................................

........................................................................................

But you actually arrived on:

........................................................................................

........................................................................................

........................................................................................

........................................................................................

Which means that astrologically, your sign is:

........................................................................................

........................................................................................

........................................................................................

........................................................................................

# As My Due Date Got Closer

I was concerned that:

..............................................................................................

..............................................................................................

..............................................................................................

..............................................................................................

..............................................................................................

..............................................................................................

My hope was that the experience would be:

..............................................................................................

..............................................................................................

..............................................................................................

..............................................................................................

..............................................................................................

..............................................................................................

Keep track of your growing belly with photos—you won't want to forget this!

# My Labor Began

When my water broke I was:

........................................................................................

........................................................................................

........................................................................................

........................................................................................

........................................................................................

........................................................................................

I first felt labor pains when:

........................................................................................

........................................................................................

........................................................................................

........................................................................................

........................................................................................

........................................................................................

What I wore to the hospital:

..................................................................................................................
..................................................................................................................
..................................................................................................................
..................................................................................................................
..................................................................................................................
..................................................................................................................
..................................................................................................................
..................................................................................................................

What I brought for you:

..................................................................................................................
..................................................................................................................
..................................................................................................................
..................................................................................................................
..................................................................................................................
..................................................................................................................
..................................................................................................................
..................................................................................................................
..................................................................................................................

# Labor . . .

How long, how much, how quickly I forgot:

..................................................................................................................................
..................................................................................................................................
..................................................................................................................................
..................................................................................................................................
..................................................................................................................................
..................................................................................................................................
..................................................................................................................................

Who else was in the room?

..................................................................................................................................
..................................................................................................................................
..................................................................................................................................
..................................................................................................................................
..................................................................................................................................
..................................................................................................................................

What I remember most about the experience:

..............................................................................................................................

..............................................................................................................................

..............................................................................................................................

..............................................................................................................................

..............................................................................................................................

..............................................................................................................................

My birth story:

..............................................................................................................................

..............................................................................................................................

..............................................................................................................................

..............................................................................................................................

..............................................................................................................................

..............................................................................................................................

..............................................................................................................................

..............................................................................................................................

..............................................................................................................................

..............................................................................................................................

..............................................................................................................................

..............................................................................................................................

# And Then There You Were!

Who else was there when you were born:

..................................................................................................

..................................................................................................

..................................................................................................

..................................................................................................

..................................................................................................

..................................................................................................

How did they react?

..................................................................................................

..................................................................................................

..................................................................................................

..................................................................................................

..................................................................................................

..................................................................................................

Anyone filming or taking pictures?

..........................................................................................................

..........................................................................................................

..........................................................................................................

What time it was when you appeared:

..........................................................................................................

..........................................................................................................

..........................................................................................................

*Add in pictures of
your newborn baby*

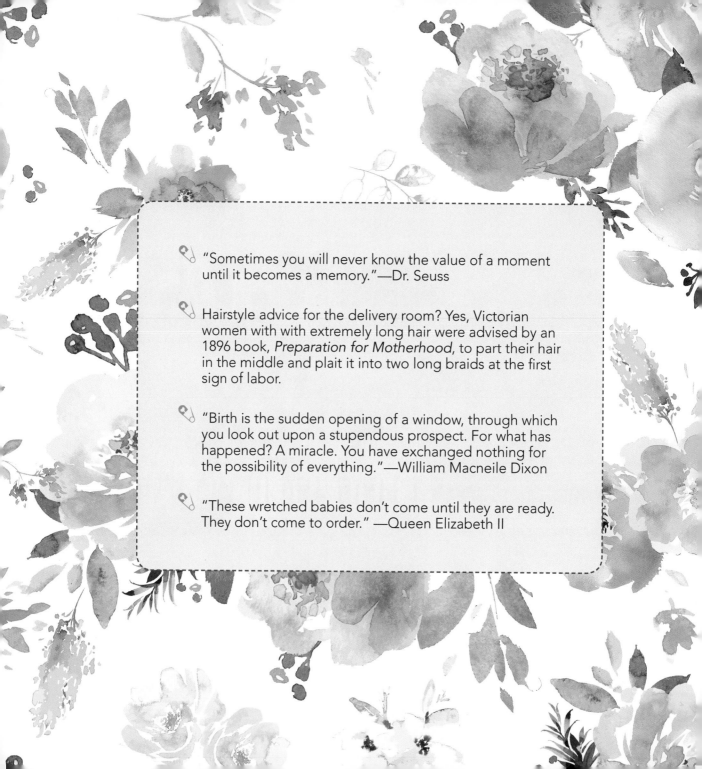

"Sometimes you will never know the value of a moment until it becomes a memory."—Dr. Seuss

Hairstyle advice for the delivery room? Yes, Victorian women with with extremely long hair were advised by an 1896 book, *Preparation for Motherhood*, to part their hair in the middle and plait it into two long braids at the first sign of labor.

"Birth is the sudden opening of a window, through which you look out upon a stupendous prospect. For what has happened? A miracle. You have exchanged nothing for the possibility of everything."—William Macneile Dixon

"These wretched babies don't come until they are ready. They don't come to order." —Queen Elizabeth II

# The First Time I Held You in My Arms

I looked into your eyes and thought:

........................................................................................................................

........................................................................................................................

........................................................................................................................

........................................................................................................................

........................................................................................................................

........................................................................................................................

Who else got to hold you:

........................................................................................................................

........................................................................................................................

........................................................................................................................

........................................................................................................................

........................................................................................................................

........................................................................................................................

# Birth Measurements

You were this big:

.................................................................................................

.................................................................................................

.................................................................................................

.................................................................................................

You weighed this much:

.................................................................................................

.................................................................................................

.................................................................................................

.................................................................................................

The doctors and nurses said that you were:

.................................................................................................

.................................................................................................

.................................................................................................

.................................................................................................

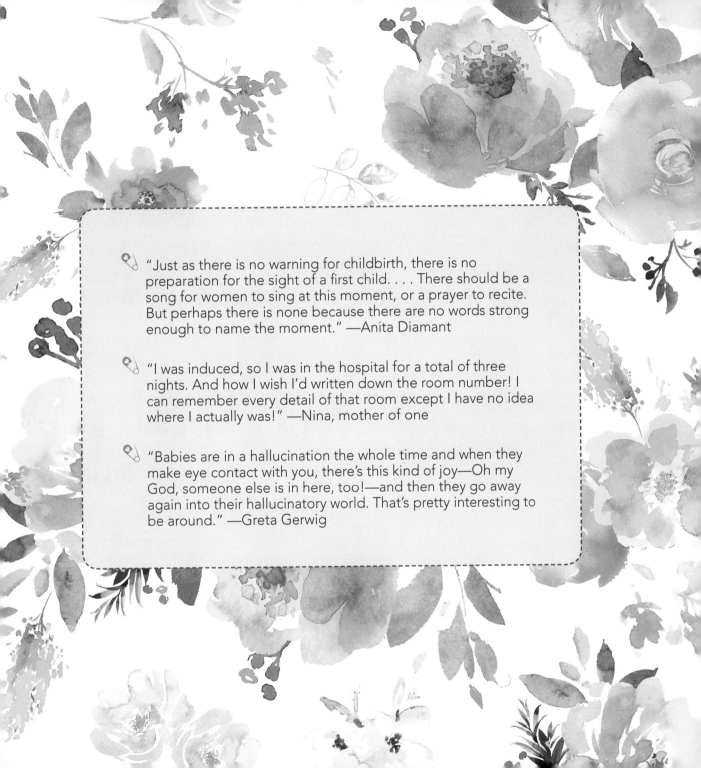

"Just as there is no warning for childbirth, there is no preparation for the sight of a first child. . . . There should be a song for women to sing at this moment, or a prayer to recite. But perhaps there is none because there are no words strong enough to name the moment." —Anita Diamant

"I was induced, so I was in the hospital for a total of three nights. And how I wish I'd written down the room number! I can remember every detail of that room except I have no idea where I actually was!" —Nina, mother of one

"Babies are in a hallucination the whole time and when they make eye contact with you, there's this kind of joy—Oh my God, someone else is in here, too!—and then they go away again into their hallucinatory world. That's pretty interesting to be around." —Greta Gerwig

*Photos of friends and family meeting baby*

# Our Night in the Hospital

Are there any specific details you remember about the hospital room?

..................................................................................................

..................................................................................................

..................................................................................................

..................................................................................................

..................................................................................................

..................................................................................................

Anything else that stands out about your stay?

..................................................................................................

..................................................................................................

..................................................................................................

..................................................................................................

..................................................................................................

..................................................................................................

# Who Came to See You in the Hospital

Baby's first visitors:

....................................................................................................................

....................................................................................................................

....................................................................................................................

....................................................................................................................

Comments and compliments:

....................................................................................................................

....................................................................................................................

....................................................................................................................

....................................................................................................................

"You look just like . . . "

....................................................................................................................

....................................................................................................................

....................................................................................................................

....................................................................................................................

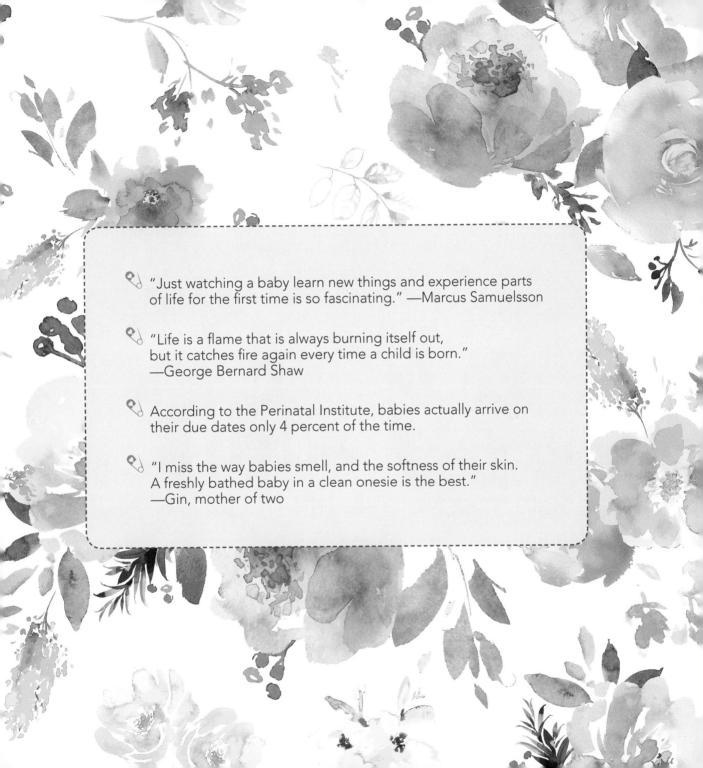

"Just watching a baby learn new things and experience parts of life for the first time is so fascinating." —Marcus Samuelsson

"Life is a flame that is always burning itself out, but it catches fire again every time a child is born." —George Bernard Shaw

According to the Perinatal Institute, babies actually arrive on their due dates only 4 percent of the time.

"I miss the way babies smell, and the softness of their skin. A freshly bathed baby in a clean onesie is the best." —Gin, mother of two

# Here is the Family You Were Brought Into

Mother:

..................................................................................................................

Father:

..................................................................................................................

Grandparents:

..................................................................................................................

Siblings:

..................................................................................................................

Aunts:

..................................................................................................................

Uncles:

..................................................................................................................

Cousins:

..................................................................................................................

*Fill in this family tree as much or as little as you like. You can write names, include photos, or choose anything else that's meaningful to you.*

*Add a photo of baby's first home here*

# Your First Home

The town where you were born:

..........................................................................................................

..........................................................................................................

..........................................................................................................

..........................................................................................................

..........................................................................................................

..........................................................................................................

The place we call home:

..........................................................................................................

..........................................................................................................

..........................................................................................................

..........................................................................................................

..........................................................................................................

..........................................................................................................

# Reflections: Your Birth

.................................................................................................................

.................................................................................................................

.................................................................................................................

.................................................................................................................

.................................................................................................................

.................................................................................................................

.................................................................................................................

.................................................................................................................

.................................................................................................................

.................................................................................................................

.................................................................................................................

.................................................................................................................

.................................................................................................................

.................................................................................................................

# Your Birth Announcement

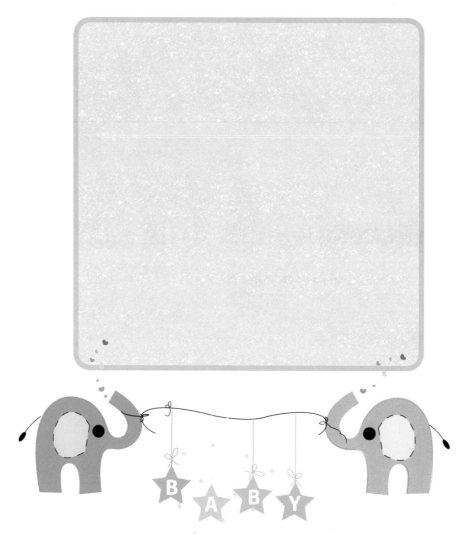

# Adjustment

Your first year.

# You Came Home from the Hospital

Your first outfit was:

..........................................................................

..........................................................................

..........................................................................

..........................................................................

..........................................................................

..........................................................................

That first night:

..........................................................................

..........................................................................

..........................................................................

..........................................................................

..........................................................................

..........................................................................

*Add a picture of baby coming home from the hospital here*

# Our First Few Days

The biggest adjustment was:

.................................................................................................................

.................................................................................................................

.................................................................................................................

.................................................................................................................

.................................................................................................................

.................................................................................................................

Some helping hands arrived:

.................................................................................................................

.................................................................................................................

.................................................................................................................

.................................................................................................................

.................................................................................................................

.................................................................................................................

# Your Sleeping Habits

Your best times of day were:

......................................................................................................

......................................................................................................

......................................................................................................

......................................................................................................

......................................................................................................

......................................................................................................

But you could never sleep when:

......................................................................................................

......................................................................................................

......................................................................................................

......................................................................................................

......................................................................................................

......................................................................................................

# Your Eating Habits

You started solid food when you were:

.............................................................................................................

.............................................................................................................

.............................................................................................................

.............................................................................................................

Your favorite food was:

.............................................................................................................

.............................................................................................................

.............................................................................................................

.............................................................................................................

You really disliked:

.............................................................................................................

.............................................................................................................

.............................................................................................................

.............................................................................................................

*Surely you have some funny photos of
baby trying new foods!*

🧷 "We moms spend so much time questioning ourselves—at least I did. We need time to just quiet those voices in our heads." —Dr. Jill Biden

🧷 Baby pacifiers have existed for thousands of years but have changed and evolved over time. Early pacifiers were made variously from bone, coral, ivory, pearl, even gold and silver. The pacifier as we know it today dates from around 1900.

🧷 "My little piece of heaven occurred during the 3:00 a.m. feedings when the rest of the world was asleep. It was just me and this perfect creature in our own little cocoon of a wicker rocking chair." —Jeanette, mother of two

🧷 "Sometimes the hardest part of parenting is allowing ourselves to be silly." —Dr. Becky Kennedy

# What Happened to My Body?

My body was different after having a baby:

..........................................................................................................................

..........................................................................................................................

..........................................................................................................................

..........................................................................................................................

..........................................................................................................................

..........................................................................................................................

The biggest change was:

..........................................................................................................................

..........................................................................................................................

..........................................................................................................................

..........................................................................................................................

..........................................................................................................................

..........................................................................................................................

# Your Favorite Toys

You loved to hold your:

..............................................................................................

..............................................................................................

..............................................................................................

..............................................................................................

Stuffed animals you had:

..............................................................................................

..............................................................................................

..............................................................................................

..............................................................................................

Toys that came as gifts:

..............................................................................................

..............................................................................................

..............................................................................................

..............................................................................................

# As for Naps . . .

While you were napping, I spent my time:

.............................................................................................................................

.............................................................................................................................

.............................................................................................................................

.............................................................................................................................

.............................................................................................................................

.............................................................................................................................

.............................................................................................................................

.............................................................................................................................

.............................................................................................................................

.............................................................................................................................

.............................................................................................................................

.............................................................................................................................

.............................................................................................................................

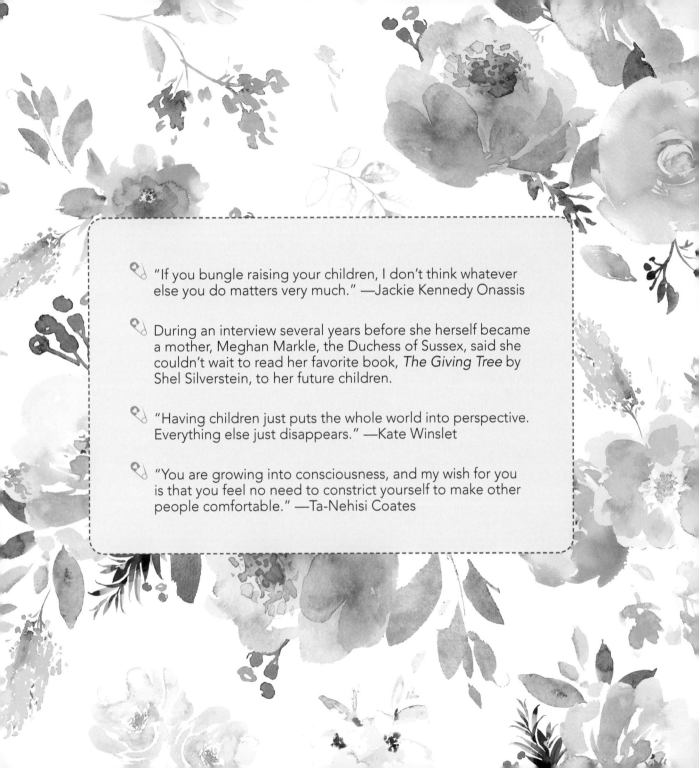

"If you bungle raising your children, I don't think whatever else you do matters very much." —Jackie Kennedy Onassis

During an interview several years before she herself became a mother, Meghan Markle, the Duchess of Sussex, said she couldn't wait to read her favorite book, *The Giving Tree* by Shel Silverstein, to her future children.

"Having children just puts the whole world into perspective. Everything else just disappears." —Kate Winslet

"You are growing into consciousness, and my wish for you is that you feel no need to constrict yourself to make other people comfortable." —Ta-Nehisi Coates

# Furry Family Members

Our pets:

..............................................................................................................

..............................................................................................................

..............................................................................................................

..............................................................................................................

..............................................................................................................

..............................................................................................................

How you all got along:

..............................................................................................................

..............................................................................................................

..............................................................................................................

..............................................................................................................

..............................................................................................................

..............................................................................................................

# Your First Steps

Early attempts:

..............................................................................................................

..............................................................................................................

..............................................................................................................

..............................................................................................................

Where you were:

..............................................................................................................

..............................................................................................................

..............................................................................................................

..............................................................................................................

Who else was there:

..............................................................................................................

..............................................................................................................

..............................................................................................................

..............................................................................................................

# Your First Words

Your first word was:

........................................................................................................

........................................................................................................

........................................................................................................

........................................................................................................

........................................................................................................

........................................................................................................

Who else heard it:

........................................................................................................

........................................................................................................

........................................................................................................

........................................................................................................

........................................................................................................

........................................................................................................

........................................................................................................

# Your First Smile

You were smiling because:

.......................................................................................................................

.......................................................................................................................

.......................................................................................................................

.......................................................................................................................

.......................................................................................................................

.......................................................................................................................

.......................................................................................................................

.......................................................................................................................

.......................................................................................................................

.......................................................................................................................

.......................................................................................................................

.......................................................................................................................

# Your First Laugh

What made you laugh:

......................................................................................................

......................................................................................................

......................................................................................................

......................................................................................................

......................................................................................................

......................................................................................................

......................................................................................................

......................................................................................................

......................................................................................................

......................................................................................................

......................................................................................................

......................................................................................................

# Monthly Milestones through Your First Year

You are one month old!

......................................................................................
......................................................................................
......................................................................................
......................................................................................

You are two months old!

......................................................................................
......................................................................................
......................................................................................
......................................................................................

You are three months old!

......................................................................................
......................................................................................
......................................................................................
......................................................................................

You are four months old!

.................................................................................................

.................................................................................................

.................................................................................................

.................................................................................................

.................................................................................................

You are five months old!

.................................................................................................

.................................................................................................

.................................................................................................

.................................................................................................

.................................................................................................

You are six months old!

.................................................................................................

.................................................................................................

.................................................................................................

.................................................................................................

.................................................................................................

You are seven months old!

.......................................................................................................................

.......................................................................................................................

.......................................................................................................................

.......................................................................................................................

.......................................................................................................................

You are eight months old!

.......................................................................................................................

.......................................................................................................................

.......................................................................................................................

.......................................................................................................................

.......................................................................................................................

You are nine months old!

.......................................................................................................................

.......................................................................................................................

.......................................................................................................................

.......................................................................................................................

.......................................................................................................................

You are ten months old!

..................................................................................................................................
..................................................................................................................................
..................................................................................................................................
..................................................................................................................................
..................................................................................................................................

You are eleven months old!

..................................................................................................................................
..................................................................................................................................
..................................................................................................................................
..................................................................................................................................
..................................................................................................................................

You are one year old!

..................................................................................................................................
..................................................................................................................................
..................................................................................................................................
..................................................................................................................................
..................................................................................................................................

# Reflections: Our First Year Together

As I look back on these past twelve months, what stands out the most to me is:

..................................................................................................
..................................................................................................
..................................................................................................
..................................................................................................
..................................................................................................
..................................................................................................
..................................................................................................
..................................................................................................
..................................................................................................
..................................................................................................
..................................................................................................
..................................................................................................
..................................................................................................

The best part of being your mother is:

..................................................................................................................................

..................................................................................................................................

..................................................................................................................................

..................................................................................................................................

..................................................................................................................................

..................................................................................................................................

..................................................................................................................................

What has most surprised me about my first year as your mother:

..................................................................................................................................

..................................................................................................................................

..................................................................................................................................

..................................................................................................................................

..................................................................................................................................

..................................................................................................................................

..................................................................................................................................

..................................................................................................................................

..................................................................................................................................

# Adventures

These early years are flying by!
Here are a few of the fun things we are doing together . . .

# You Became Your Own Person

Early signs of independence:

........................................................................................

........................................................................................

........................................................................................

........................................................................................

........................................................................................

........................................................................................

Your personality emerged:

........................................................................................

........................................................................................

........................................................................................

........................................................................................

........................................................................................

........................................................................................

Add photos of your child
with early friends

# Your First Friends

Some of your earliest friends were:

...................................................................................................................................

...................................................................................................................................

...................................................................................................................................

...................................................................................................................................

...................................................................................................................................

...................................................................................................................................

How you met them:

...................................................................................................................................

...................................................................................................................................

...................................................................................................................................

...................................................................................................................................

...................................................................................................................................

...................................................................................................................................

...................................................................................................................................

# Your Favorite Playgrounds

The equipment you loved the most:

..........................................................................................

..........................................................................................

..........................................................................................

..........................................................................................

..........................................................................................

..........................................................................................

But you didn't really like:

..........................................................................................

..........................................................................................

..........................................................................................

..........................................................................................

..........................................................................................

..........................................................................................

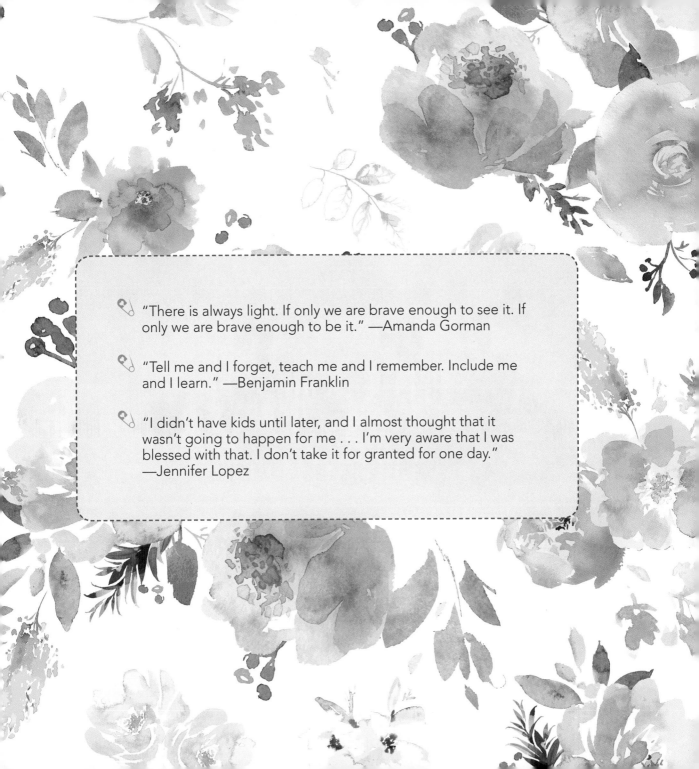

"There is always light. If only we are brave enough to see it. If only we are brave enough to be it." —Amanda Gorman

"Tell me and I forget, teach me and I remember. Include me and I learn." —Benjamin Franklin

"I didn't have kids until later, and I almost thought that it wasn't going to happen for me . . . I'm very aware that I was blessed with that. I don't take it for granted for one day." —Jennifer Lopez

# Day Care and Nursery School Years

What age did you start going to day care or school?

..................................................................................................................

..................................................................................................................

..................................................................................................................

..................................................................................................................

Who else was there?

..................................................................................................................

..................................................................................................................

..................................................................................................................

..................................................................................................................

Who was in charge?

..................................................................................................................

..................................................................................................................

..................................................................................................................

..................................................................................................................

*Add in school photos through the years*

# Your Preschool

Your daily activities were:

........................................................................................................

........................................................................................................

........................................................................................................

........................................................................................................

........................................................................................................

........................................................................................................

........................................................................................................

........................................................................................................

........................................................................................................

........................................................................................................

........................................................................................................

........................................................................................................

# Learning to Read

You learned to read by:

........................................................................................................

........................................................................................................

........................................................................................................

........................................................................................................

Your favorite books were:

........................................................................................................

........................................................................................................

........................................................................................................

........................................................................................................

Your favorite time to read or be read to:

........................................................................................................

........................................................................................................

........................................................................................................

........................................................................................................

# Our Family Vacations

Where we went, when, and why:

........................................................................................................

........................................................................................................

........................................................................................................

........................................................................................................

........................................................................................................

........................................................................................................

........................................................................................................

........................................................................................................

........................................................................................................

........................................................................................................

........................................................................................................

........................................................................................................

*You'll always cherish these precious memories; document them in this moment so you don't forget*

"The best candy shop a child can be left alone in is the library." —Maya Angelou

Long distance road travel is a classic family vacation, particularly around the major holidays. According to AAA, only 10 percent of travelers fly for the Thanksgiving holiday, with 90 percent choosing to drive.

"I confess, now that my daughter is older, I miss being able to look in the rearview mirror and see her strapped safely in her car seat." —Jen, mother of one

"You're in a constant state of worrying about your children. It's very painful and it's exhilarating. It's a really interesting way of living in the world. It's what I wanted and with that, though, comes witnessing somebody hopefully develop into a really interesting, decent person who contributes something." —Sarah Jessica Parker

# Our Pet Family

Dogs, cats, or any other beloved pets we had while you were growing up:

.........................................................................................................................

.........................................................................................................................

.........................................................................................................................

.........................................................................................................................

.........................................................................................................................

.........................................................................................................................

.........................................................................................................................

.........................................................................................................................

.........................................................................................................................

.........................................................................................................................

.........................................................................................................................

.........................................................................................................................

.........................................................................................................................

.........................................................................................................................

*Include photos of your
child with furry friends*

# Your Interests and Hobbies

You really liked:

..................................................................................................

..................................................................................................

..................................................................................................

..................................................................................................

..................................................................................................

..................................................................................................

You lost interest in:

..................................................................................................

..................................................................................................

..................................................................................................

..................................................................................................

..................................................................................................

..................................................................................................

Your favorite movies:

......................................................................................................
......................................................................................................
......................................................................................................
......................................................................................................
......................................................................................................
......................................................................................................
......................................................................................................
......................................................................................................

Your favorite music:

......................................................................................................
......................................................................................................
......................................................................................................
......................................................................................................
......................................................................................................
......................................................................................................
......................................................................................................
......................................................................................................

# Your First Road Trip

We went to:

...................................................................................................................

...................................................................................................................

...................................................................................................................

...................................................................................................................

...................................................................................................................

...................................................................................................................

How we got there:

...................................................................................................................

...................................................................................................................

...................................................................................................................

...................................................................................................................

...................................................................................................................

...................................................................................................................

# Your First Plane Trip

We flew to:

..................................................................................................................................
..................................................................................................................................
..................................................................................................................................
..................................................................................................................................
..................................................................................................................................
..................................................................................................................................

Why we went there:

..................................................................................................................................
..................................................................................................................................
..................................................................................................................................
..................................................................................................................................
..................................................................................................................................
..................................................................................................................................

# Your First Restaurant Experience

We went to:

...........................................................................................

...........................................................................................

...........................................................................................

...........................................................................................

...........................................................................................

...........................................................................................

What you ate:

...........................................................................................

...........................................................................................

...........................................................................................

...........................................................................................

...........................................................................................

...........................................................................................

# Outdoor Adventures

Neighborhood backyards and parks:

..................................................................................................

..................................................................................................

..................................................................................................

Family camping trips:

..................................................................................................

..................................................................................................

..................................................................................................

Afternoon walks and hikes:

..................................................................................................

..................................................................................................

..................................................................................................

Beach trips:

..................................................................................................

..................................................................................................

..................................................................................................

# Your Height and Weight Records

Age One:

........................................................................................................

........................................................................................................

Age Two:

........................................................................................................

........................................................................................................

Age Three:

........................................................................................................

........................................................................................................

Age Four:

........................................................................................................

........................................................................................................

Age Five:

........................................................................................................

........................................................................................................

Age Six:

.....................................................................................................................................

.....................................................................................................................................

Age Seven:

.....................................................................................................................................

.....................................................................................................................................

Age Eight:

.....................................................................................................................................

.....................................................................................................................................

Age Nine:

.....................................................................................................................................

.....................................................................................................................................

Age Ten:

.....................................................................................................................................

.....................................................................................................................................

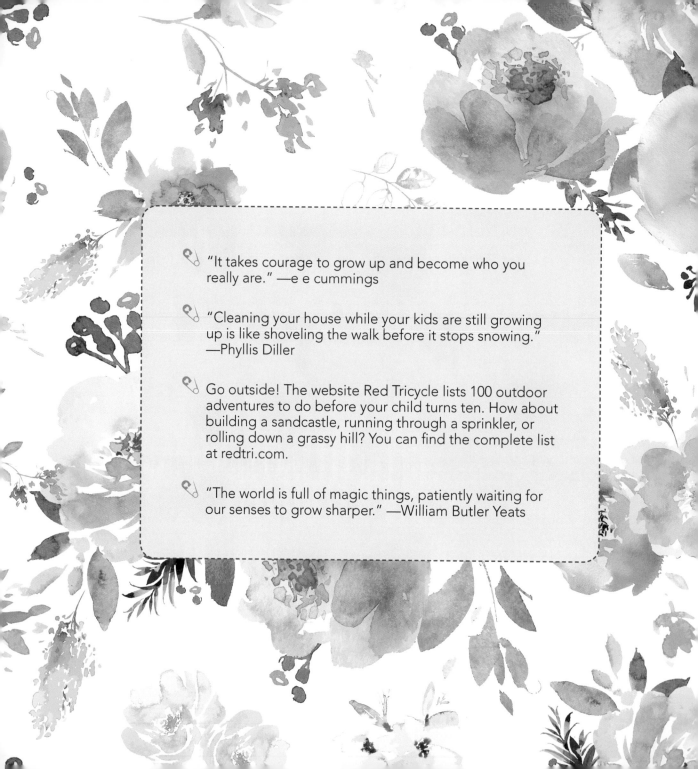

"It takes courage to grow up and become who you really are." —e e cummings

"Cleaning your house while your kids are still growing up is like shoveling the walk before it stops snowing." —Phyllis Diller

Go outside! The website Red Tricycle lists 100 outdoor adventures to do before your child turns ten. How about building a sandcastle, running through a sprinkler, or rolling down a grassy hill? You can find the complete list at redtri.com.

"The world is full of magic things, patiently waiting for our senses to grow sharper." —William Butler Yeats

# A Few Bumps and Scrapes

Any childhood illnesses:

........................................................................................................

........................................................................................................

........................................................................................................

........................................................................................................

........................................................................................................

........................................................................................................

Ouch! You hurt yourself:

........................................................................................................

........................................................................................................

........................................................................................................

........................................................................................................

........................................................................................................

........................................................................................................

# Your School Years

Grade school highlights:

........................................................................................................

........................................................................................................

........................................................................................................

........................................................................................................

Junior high highlights:

........................................................................................................

........................................................................................................

........................................................................................................

........................................................................................................

High school highlights:

........................................................................................................

........................................................................................................

........................................................................................................

........................................................................................................

# Fun School Stuff

Dances and proms you attended:

..............................................................................................................

..............................................................................................................

..............................................................................................................

..............................................................................................................

..............................................................................................................

..............................................................................................................

..............................................................................................................

Sports activities you took part in:

..............................................................................................................

..............................................................................................................

..............................................................................................................

..............................................................................................................

..............................................................................................................

..............................................................................................................

..............................................................................................................

# Your Report Cards

Positive teacher comments:

................................................................................................................................

................................................................................................................................

................................................................................................................................

................................................................................................................................

................................................................................................................................

................................................................................................................................

................................................................................................................................

But there was room for improvement:

................................................................................................................................

................................................................................................................................

................................................................................................................................

................................................................................................................................

................................................................................................................................

................................................................................................................................

................................................................................................................................

*Add in a report card*

# Birthdays

How we celebrated your birthday:

.............................................................................................................................

.............................................................................................................................

.............................................................................................................................

.............................................................................................................................

Any specially themed parties:

.............................................................................................................................

.............................................................................................................................

.............................................................................................................................

.............................................................................................................................

Your favorite party:

.............................................................................................................................

.............................................................................................................................

.............................................................................................................................

.............................................................................................................................

# Reflections: Through the Years

There may have been some bumps in the road . . .

............................................................................................

............................................................................................

............................................................................................

............................................................................................

............................................................................................

............................................................................................

............................................................................................

............................................................................................

............................................................................................

............................................................................................

............................................................................................

............................................................................................

# Reflections: Precious Memories

As I look back on your early years, what stays with me the most is . . .

...........................................................................................................................

...........................................................................................................................

...........................................................................................................................

...........................................................................................................................

...........................................................................................................................

...........................................................................................................................

...........................................................................................................................

...........................................................................................................................

...........................................................................................................................

...........................................................................................................................

...........................................................................................................................

...........................................................................................................................

...........................................................................................................................

# More about Mama

Okay, now what about you? Have you included much of yourself and your pre-motherhood life in these pages? Are there things you'd like your baby to know someday?

In the coming decades, you, Mom, will be the keeper of this book. As a way to reconnect with your child's early years, as a way to embarrass them in front of their friends, as a way to double-check your fading recollections. But this memory book will one day become a keepsake for your grown children, and their children, and so on. So why not take a few pages here to write a message to your future descendants?

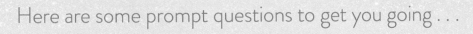

Here are some prompt questions to get you going . . .

Did you have a baby book from your own early years? If so, do you still have it?

..........................................................................................................................

..........................................................................................................................

..........................................................................................................................

..........................................................................................................................

..........................................................................................................................

..........................................................................................................................

..........................................................................................................................

What were your first words?

..........................................................................................................................

..........................................................................................................................

..........................................................................................................................

..........................................................................................................................

..........................................................................................................................

..........................................................................................................................

..........................................................................................................................

Where did you take your first steps?

........................................................................................................

........................................................................................................

........................................................................................................

........................................................................................................

........................................................................................................

........................................................................................................

........................................................................................................

What can you pass along from what your mother wrote about your early years?

........................................................................................................

........................................................................................................

........................................................................................................

........................................................................................................

........................................................................................................

........................................................................................................

........................................................................................................

When did you learn to walk?

..................................................................................................
..................................................................................................
..................................................................................................
..................................................................................................
..................................................................................................
..................................................................................................
..................................................................................................

Do you still have mementos from your childhood that your mother kept? A knitted cap? Baby socks? Do you hope to pass those along for future generations to use?

..................................................................................................
..................................................................................................
..................................................................................................
..................................................................................................
..................................................................................................
..................................................................................................
..................................................................................................

A blank page is daunting. Maybe you can doodle a bit on the edges of the page in order to get your creativity and imagination flowing. And years from now someone else will discover your little drawings and smile.

Worried that no one will want to hear about your life or your experiences? Rest assured, they will. Just as you are curious about who came before you and what their lives were like, so too will your story interest those who read it in the future.

No need to fill up this mama memoir section in one sitting. Start and stop whenever the mood strikes. Take years to do it at all, if you want!

What are your earliest memories from childhood?

..........................................................................................................

..........................................................................................................

..........................................................................................................

..........................................................................................................

..........................................................................................................

..........................................................................................................

..........................................................................................................

Do you have a clear mental picture of where you lived in your early years?

..........................................................................................................

..........................................................................................................

..........................................................................................................

..........................................................................................................

..........................................................................................................

..........................................................................................................

..........................................................................................................

Did you have older brothers and sisters? Any younger siblings? What can you remember about those years?

....................................................................................................................

....................................................................................................................

....................................................................................................................

....................................................................................................................

....................................................................................................................

....................................................................................................................

Why did your parents give you your name? Are you named after a family member or a beloved friend? Did you have a nickname growing up?

....................................................................................................................

....................................................................................................................

....................................................................................................................

....................................................................................................................

....................................................................................................................

....................................................................................................................

What were your favorite foods as a child? Who made them for you?

......................................................................................................................................
......................................................................................................................................
......................................................................................................................................
......................................................................................................................................
......................................................................................................................................
......................................................................................................................................
......................................................................................................................................

Do you remember your grandparents? Anyone else from earlier generations?

......................................................................................................................................
......................................................................................................................................
......................................................................................................................................
......................................................................................................................................
......................................................................................................................................
......................................................................................................................................

Is there a family health history that you want to pass along for the next generation?

.......................................................................................................................................

.......................................................................................................................................

.......................................................................................................................................

.......................................................................................................................................

.......................................................................................................................................

.......................................................................................................................................

.......................................................................................................................................

The story that you tell most from your own childhood is:

.......................................................................................................................................

.......................................................................................................................................

.......................................................................................................................................

.......................................................................................................................................

.......................................................................................................................................

.......................................................................................................................................

.......................................................................................................................................

Is there a trait or talent that you inherited from your parents?

.......................................................................................................

.......................................................................................................

.......................................................................................................

.......................................................................................................

.......................................................................................................

.......................................................................................................

.......................................................................................................

Did your family have pets while you were growing up? Did you have a favorite?

.......................................................................................................

.......................................................................................................

.......................................................................................................

.......................................................................................................

.......................................................................................................

.......................................................................................................

.......................................................................................................

What was your most memorable family vacation? Who else was with you?

...........................................................................................................................

...........................................................................................................................

...........................................................................................................................

...........................................................................................................................

...........................................................................................................................

...........................................................................................................................

...........................................................................................................................

What has stayed with you from your school experiences? Favorite school, subject, or teacher?

...........................................................................................................................

...........................................................................................................................

...........................................................................................................................

...........................................................................................................................

...........................................................................................................................

...........................................................................................................................

...........................................................................................................................

In what way do you resemble your own parents? In what ways are you different?

........................................................................................................

........................................................................................................

........................................................................................................

........................................................................................................

........................................................................................................

........................................................................................................

........................................................................................................

Is there a message that you'd like to pass along to anyone reading this memory journal in the future?

........................................................................................................

........................................................................................................

........................................................................................................

........................................................................................................

........................................................................................................

........................................................................................................

........................................................................................................

Copyright © 2021 by Jennifer Basye Sander

All rights reserved. No part of this book may be reproduced in any manner without the express written consent of the publisher, except in the case of brief excerpts in critical reviews or articles. All inquiries should be addressed to Skyhorse Publishing, 307 West 36th Street, 11th Floor, New York, NY 10018.

Skyhorse Publishing books may be purchased in bulk at special discounts for sales promotion, corporate gifts, fund-raising, or educational purposes. Special editions can also be created to specifications. For details, contact the Special Sales Department, Skyhorse Publishing, 307 West 36th Street, 11th Floor, New York, NY 10018 or info@skyhorsepublishing.com.

Skyhorse® and Skyhorse Publishing® are registered trademarks of Skyhorse Publishing, Inc.®, a Delaware corporation.

Visit our website at www.skyhorsepublishing.com.

10 9 8 7 6 5 4 3 2 1

Library of Congress Cataloging-in-Publication Data is available on file.

Cover design by Laura Klynstra

Interior design by Chris Schultz

Edited by Leah Zarra

ISBN: 978-1-5107-6538-2

Printed in China